LET'S *do* BRUNCH

D1512220

LET'S *do* BRUNCH

Mouth-Watering Meals to Start Your Day

STERLING EPICURE
New York

STERLING EPICURE
New York

An Imprint of Sterling Publishing
387 Park Avenue South
New York, NY 10016

First published in the United Kingdom in 2013 by
Pavilion Books Company Limited

ISBN 978-1-4549-1524-9

For information about custom editions, special
sales, and premium and corporate purchases,
please contact Sterling Special Sales at 800-805-
5489 or specialsales@sterlingpublishing.com.

Manufactured in China

10 9 8 7 6 5 4 3 2 1

www.sterlingpublishing.com

NOTES
All spoon measures are level.

Ovens and broilers must be preheated to the
specified temperature.

Large eggs should be used except where otherwise
specified. Free-range eggs are recommended.

All-purpose, bread, self-rising, and wholewheat
flours should unsifted and spooned into the cup
measure and then leveled.

Note that some recipes contain raw or lightly
cooked eggs. The young, elderly, pregnant women
and anyone with an immune-deficiency disease
should avoid these because of the slight risk
of salmonella.

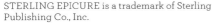

Contents

Cereal and Fruit

Toasted Oats with Berries

Prep time: 10 minutes
Cooking time: about 10 minutes, plus cooling

2 tbsp. roughly chopped hazelnuts

1⅓ cups rolled oats

1 tbsp. olive oil

¾ cup sliced strawberries

1⅔ cups blueberries

¾ cup plus 2 tbsp. Greek-style yogurt

2 tbsp. honey

1 Heat the broiler to medium. Put the hazelnuts into a bowl with the oats. Drizzle with the oil and mix well, then spread out on a baking sheet. Toast the oat mixture for 5–10 minutes under the broiler until it starts to crisp. Remove from the heat and let cool.

2 Put the strawberries into a large bowl with the blueberries and yogurt. Stir in the oats and hazelnuts, drizzle with the honey, and divide among four dishes. Serve immediately.

TRY THIS

If you don't have any strawberries or blueberries on hand, substitute with other fruits, such as raspberries, blackberries, and chopped nectarines or peaches.

Serves 4

Granola

Prep time: 5 minutes
Cooking time: 1 hour 5 minutes

3⅓ cups rolled oats

4 tbsp. each chopped Brazil nuts, slivered almonds, wheat germ or rye flakes, and sunflower seeds

2 tbsp. sesame seeds

7 tbsp. sunflower oil

3 tbsp. honey

⅔ cup each raisins and dried cranberries

milk or yogurt to serve

HEALTHY TIP

Granola is an excellent breakfast option because the oats provide a sustained rise in blood sugar, helping to keep hunger at bay longer. Brazil nuts used in this recipe are rich in selenium, a powerful antioxidant nutrient, while the almonds supply valuable amounts of bone-building calcium, protein, and zinc.

1 Heat the oven to 275°F (250°F for convection ovens). Put the oats, nuts, wheatgerm, or rye flakes, and all the seeds into a bowl. Gently heat the oil and honey in a pan. Pour over the oats mixture and stir to combine. Spread on a shallow baking tray and bake in the oven for 1 hour, or until golden, stirring once. Let cool.

2 Transfer to a large bowl and stir in the raisins and dried cranberries. Store in an airtight container—the granola will keep for up to a week. Serve with milk or yogurt.

Makes 15 servings

Oatmeal with Dried Fruit

Prep time: 5 minutes
Cooking time: 5 minutes

2¼ cups oatmeal

1¾ cups (400ml) milk, plus extra
  to serve

¾ cup mixture of chopped dried figs,
  apricots, and raisins

1 Put the oatmeal into a large pan and add the milk and 1¾ cups (400ml) water. Stir in the figs, apricots, and raisins and heat gently, stirring until the mixture thickens and the oatmeal is cooked.

2 Divide among four bowls and serve with a splash of milk.

Serves 4

Muesli bars

Some of the simplest cookies to make are bar cookies, which are baked in one piece and then cut into bars. The mixtures often contain fruit, nuts, and oats.

To make 12 bars, you will need: 1½ sticks unsalted butter, cut into pieces, ⅔ cup packed light brown sugar, 2 tbsp. Lyle's Golden Syrup, heaped 4 cups rolled oats, ⅔ cup roughly chopped ready-to-eat dried papaya, ⅓ cup golden raisins, ½ cup roughly chopped pecans, 2 tbsp. roughly chopped pine nuts, 2 tbsp. pumpkin seeds, 1 tbsp. all-purpose flour, and 1 tsp. ground cinnamon.

1. Heat the oven to 350°F (300°F for convection ovens). Melt the butter, sugar, and golden syrup together in a heavy-bottomed pan over low heat.
2. Meanwhile, put the oats, dried fruit, nuts, seeds, flour, and cinnamon into a large bowl and stir to mix. Pour in the melted mixture and mix together until combined.
3. Spoon the mixture into a 12 × 8in (30 × 20cm) nonstick baking pan and press down into the corners.
4. Bake for 25–30 minutes until golden. Press the mixture down again if necessary, then use a metal spatula to mark into 12 bars.
5. Cool completely. Use a metal spatula to lift the bars out of the pan and store them in an airtight container.

EEZE AHEAD

e individually wrapped muesli
s in the freezer. Remove and
w for a couple of hours for the
ect after-school snack.

Energy-Boosting Muesli

Prep time: 5 minutes

5½ cups rolled oats

⅔ cup chopped toasted almonds

2 tbsp. pumpkin seeds

2 tbsp. sunflower seeds

⅔ cup ready-to-eat dried apricots, chopped

milk or yogurt to serve

1 Mix the oats with the almonds, seeds, and apricots. Store in a sealable container: it will keep for up to one month. Serve with milk or yogurt.

HEALTHY TIP

Dried apricots are a rich source of fiber and iron, as well as vitamins A and C.

Makes 15 servings

Apple and Almond Yogurt

Prep time: 5 minutes, plus overnight chilling

2 cups plain yogurt

⅓ cup each raisins and
  slivered almonds

2 apples

1 Put the yogurt into a bowl and add the raisins and almonds.

2 Grate the apples, add to the bowl, and mix together. Chill in the refrigerator overnight. Use as a topping for breakfast cereal or serve as a snack.

TRY THIS

If you don't have any apples, you could use pears instead. You can also replace the raisins with dried cranberries.

Serves 4

Breakfast Bruschetta

TAKE 5

🍴 **Prep time:** 5 minutes
Cooking time: 5 minutes

1 ripe banana, peeled and sliced

1⅔ cups blueberries

¾ cup plus 2 tbsp. Greek-style yogurt

4 slices pumpernickel or wheat-free
   wholegrain bread

1 tbsp. honey

1 Put the banana into a bowl with the blueberries. Spoon in the yogurt and mix well.

2 Toast the slices of bread, then spread with the blueberry mixture. Drizzle with honey and serve immediately.

HEALTHY TIP

This toasted treat is very low in fat. Pumpernickel bread is made from rye flour, which is rich in fiber, iron, and zinc. The blueberries are rich in anthocyanins, which help combat heart disease, certain cancers, and strokes.

Serves 4

Apple Compote

Prep time: 10 minutes, plus chilling
Cooking time: 5 minutes, plus cooling

2 cups peeled and chopped
  cooking apples

juice of ½ lemon

1 tbsp. sugar

ground cinnamon

2 tbsp. raisins; 2 tbsp. chopped almonds;
  1 tbsp. plain yogurt to serve

1 Put the cooking apples into a pan with the lemon juice, sugar, and 2 tbsp. cold water. Cook gently for 5 minutes, or until soft. Transfer to a bowl.

2 Sprinkle a little ground cinnamon over the top, cool, and chill. It will keep for up to three days.

3 Serve with the raisins, chopped almonds, and yogurt.

SAVE TIME

To microwave, put the apples, lemon juice, sugar, and 2 tbsp. water into a microwaveproof bowl, cover loosely with microwavesafe plastic wrap, and microwave on full power for 4 minutes or until the apples are just soft.

Serves 2

Perfect Berries

Soft fruit—strawberries, blackberries, raspberries, and currants—are generally quick to prepare. Always handle ripe fruits gently, because they can be delicate.

Washing berries

Most berries can be washed very gently in cold water. Bought blackberries will usually have the hull removed. If you have picked blackberries yourself, however, the hulls and stems can still be attached, so pick over the berries carefully and remove any that remain. Raspberries are very delicate, so handle them carefully; remove any stems and hulls. Leave strawberries whole.

1. Place the berries in a bowl of cold water and let any small pieces of grit, dust, or insects to float out.
2. Transfer the fruit to a colander and rinse gently under fresh running water. Drain well, then gently blot the fruit with paper towels until they are dry.

Hulling strawberries

1. Wash the strawberries gently and dry on paper towels. Remove the hull (the middle part that is attached to the plant) from the strawberry using a strawberry huller or a small sharp knife.

2. Put the knife into the small, hard area beneath the green stem and gently rotate to remove a small, cone-shaped piece.

Strawberry Compote

Prep time: 15 minutes, plus overnight chilling
Cooking time: 10 minutes, plus cooling

scant ½ cup raspberry preserves

juice of 1 orange

juice of 1 lemon

1 tsp. rose water

heaped 2 cups hulled and thickly
sliced strawberries

1 cup blueberries

1 Put the raspberry preserves into a pan
with the orange and lemon juices and
add 5 tbsp. (75ml) boiling water. Stir
over low heat to dissolve the mixture.
Set aside to cool.

2 Stir in the rose water and taste—you
might want to add another squeeze
of lemon juice if it's too sweet. Put
the strawberries and blueberries into
a large serving bowl, then strain the
raspberry mixture over them. Cover
and chill overnight. Remove the bowl
from the refrigerator 30 minutes
before serving.

HEALTHY TIP

Berries are densely packed with
vitamins, antioxidants, and other
phytonutrients (highly nutritious,
active compounds found in
fruit, vegetables, whole grains,
beans, legumes, nuts and seeds,
and herbs and spices). Berries
also contain compounds called
anthocyanins—the pigment that
gives berries their intense color,
mops up damaging free radicals,
and helps prevent cancer and heart
disease. Combined with vitamin C,
anthocyanins help to improve blood
flow around the body.

Exotic Fruit Salad

Prep time: 10 minutes

2 oranges, cut into segments

1 mango, peeled, pitted, and chopped (see page 156)

scant 2 cups peeled and diced fresh pineapple (see page 157)

1⅓ cups blueberries

½ cantaloupe, cubed

grated zest and juice of 1 lime

1 Put the orange segments into a bowl and add the mango, pineapple, blueberries, and cantaloupe. Add the lime zest and juice.

2 Gently mix the fruit together and serve immediately.

HEALTHY TIP

Fresh pineapple contains the enzyme bromelain, which aids digestion and is beneficial for inflammatory conditions such as sinusitis and rheumatoid arthritis.

Tropical Fruit Pots

Prep time: 15 minutes
Cooking time: 5 minutes

1 can (15-oz./425g) can apricots in fruit
   juice

2 balls of preserved ginger in syrup,
   finely chopped, plus 2 tbsp.
   syrup from the jar

½ tsp. ground cinnamon

juice of 1 orange

3 oranges, cut into segments

1 mango, peeled, pitted, and chopped
   (see page 156)

1 pineapple, peeled, core removed,
   and chopped (see page 157)

2 cups coconut-flavored yogurt

3 tbsp. lemon curd

3–4 tbsp. light brown sugar

1 Drain the juice from the apricots into
   a pan and stir in the syrup from the
   ginger. Add the chopped ginger, the
   cinnamon, and orange juice. Cook
   over low heat and stir gently. Bring
   to a boil, then reduce the heat and
   simmer for 2–3 minutes to make
   a thick syrup.

2 Roughly chop the apricots and put
   into a bowl with the segmented
   oranges, the mango, and pineapple.
   Pour the syrup over the fruit. Divide
   among eight dessert bowls or glasses.

3 Beat the yogurt and lemon curd
   together in a bowl until smooth.
   Spoon a generous dollop over the
   fruit and sprinkle with brown sugar.
   Chill if not serving immediately.

SAVE TIME

To prepare ahead, complete the
recipe to the end of step 2 up to
2 hours before you plan to eat—
there isn't any need to chill.

Serves 8

Pastries
and Muffins

Croissants

Prep time: 40 minutes, plus chilling and standing
Cooking time: 15 minutes

1oz. (25g) fresh yeast or 1 tbsp. active dry
yeast and 1 tsp. sugar

2 eggs

3¼ cups all-purpose flour, plus extra
to dust the pan

2 tsp. salt

2 tbsp. lard

2 sticks unsalted butter, at cool room
temperature

½ tsp. sugar

1 Blend the fresh yeast with 1 cup plus 1
tbsp. (250ml) tepid water. If using dry
yeast, sprinkle it into the water with
the 1 tsp. sugar and leave in a warm
place for 15 minutes, or until frothy.

2 Whisk 1 egg into the yeast liquid. Sift
the flour and salt into a large bowl
and cut in the lard. Make a well in the
middle and pour in the yeast liquid.
Mix and then beat in the flour until
the bowl is left clean. Turn out on to a
lightly floured work surface and knead
well for about 10 minutes, or until the
dough is firm and elastic.

3 Roll out the dough on a lightly
floured work surface to an oblong
about 20 × 8in. (50 × 20cm). Keep the
edges as square as possible, gently
pulling out the corners to prevent
them from curling under. Dust the
rolling pin with flour to prevent it
from sticking to the dough.

4 Divide the butter into three portions.
Dot one portion over the top two-
thirds of the dough, but clear of the
edge. Turn up the bottom third of the
dough over half the butter, then fold
down the remaining dough. Seal the
edges with a rolling pin. Turn the
dough so that the fold is on the right.

5 Press the dough lightly at intervals
along its length, then roll out into an
oblong again. Repeat the rolling and
folding with the other two portions
of butter. Rest the dough in the
refrigerator for 30 minutes, loosely
covered with a clean dish towel.
Repeat three more times, cover, and
chill for 1 hour.

6 Roll out the dough to an oblong about 19 × 13in. (47.5 × 32.5cm), lay a clean dish towel over the top, and let it rest for 10 minutes. Trim off ½in. (1cm) all around and divide the dough in half lengthwise, then into three squares, then across into triangles.

7 Beat the remaining egg, 1 tbsp. water, and the sugar together for the glaze and brush it over the triangles. Roll up each triangle from the long edge, finishing with the tip underneath. Curve into crescents and place well apart on ungreased cookie sheets, allowing room for each to spread. Cover loosely with a clean dish towel. Leave at room temperature for about 30 minutes until well risen and "puffy."

8 Heat the oven to 425°F (400°F for convection ovens). Brush each croissant carefully with more glaze. Bake for 15 minutes, or until crisp and well browned.

Croissants (see previous page)

Makes 12

Danish Pastries (see overleaf)

Makes 16

Danish Pastries

Prep time: 1 hour, plus rising and resting
Cooking time: 15 minutes

1oz. (25g) fresh yeast or 1 tbsp. active dry
   yeast and 1 tsp. sugar

3⅔ cups all-purpose flour, plus extra to
   dust the pan

1 tsp. salt

2 tbsp. lard

2 tbsp. sugar

2 eggs, beaten

2½ sticks butter, softened

1 egg, beaten, to glaze

sugar glaze (see page 48) and slivered
   almonds, to decorate

For the almond paste

1 tbsp. butter

⅓ cup superfine sugar

¾ cup almond meal

1 egg, beaten

For the cinnamon butter

4 tbsp. butter

¼ cup sugar

2 tsp. ground cinnamon

1 Blend the fresh yeast with ½ cup (125ml) tepid water. If using dry yeast, sprinkle it into the water with the 1 tsp. sugar and leave in a warm place for 15 minutes, or until frothy.

2 Mix the flour and salt, cut in the lard, and stir in the 2 tbsp. sugar. Add the yeast liquid and beaten eggs and mix to an elastic dough, adding a little more water if necessary. Knead well for 5 minutes on a lightly floured work surface until smooth. Put the dough back into the rinsed-out bowl, cover with a clean dish towel, and refrigerate for 10 minutes.

3 Shape the butter into a rectangle. Roll out the dough on a floured board to a rectangle about three times as wide as the butter. Put the butter sticks next to each other in the middle of the dough over the butter. Press the edges to seal.

4 With the folds at the sides, roll the dough into a strip three times as long as it is wide; fold the bottom third up, and the top third down, cover, and rest

for 10 minutes. Turn and repeat the rolling, folding, and resting twice more.

5 To make the almond paste, cream the butter and sugar, stir in the almonds, and add enough egg to make a soft and pliable consistency. Make the cinnamon butter by creaming the butter and sugar and beating in the cinnamon.

6 Roll out the dough into the required shapes (see below) and fill with almond paste or cinnamon butter. Cover the pastries with a clean dish towel and leave in a warm place for 20–30 minutes until doubled in size. Heat the oven to 425°F (400°F for convection ovens).

7. Brush the pastries with beaten egg. Bake for 15 minutes, or until golden. While hot, brush the pastries with sugar glaze and sprinkle with slivered almonds.

To shape the pastries

Imperial stars Cut into 3in. (7.5cm) squares. Make diagonal cuts from each corner to within ½in. (1cm) of the middle. Put a piece of almond paste in the middle. Fold one corner of each cut section down to the middle, secure the tips with beaten egg.

Foldovers and cushions Cut into 3in. (7.5cm) squares and put a little almond paste in the middle. Fold over two opposite corners to the middle. Make a cushion by folding over all four corners, securing the tips with beaten egg.

Twists Cut into 10 × 4in (25 × 10cm) rectangles. Cut each rectangle lengthwise to make four pieces. Spread with cinnamon butter and fold the bottom third of each up and the top third down; seal and cut each across into thin slices. Form into twists.

Crumpets

2¾ cups plus 1 tbsp. all-purpose flour

½ tsp. salt

½ tsp. baking soda

1½ tsp. instant dry yeast

1 cup warm milk

a little vegetable oil to fry

butter to serve

1 Sift the flour, salt, and baking soda into a large bowl and stir in the yeast. Make a well in the middle, then pour in 1 cup of warm water and the warm milk. Mix to a thick batter.

2 Using a wooden spoon, beat the batter vigorously for about 5 minutes. Cover and leave in a warm place for about 1 hour until spongelike in texture. Beat the batter for 2 minutes longer, then transfer to a pitcher.

3 Put a large, nonstick frying pan over high heat and brush a little oil over the surface. Oil the insides of four crumpet rings or 3in. (7.5cm) plain metal cutters. Put the rings, blunt-edge down, on the hot pan's surface and leave for about 2 minutes until very hot.

4 Pour a little batter into each ring to a depth of ½in. (1cm). Cook the crumpets for 4–5 minutes until the surface is set and appears honeycombed with holes.

5 Carefully remove each metal ring. Flip the crumpets over and cook the other side for 1 minute only. Transfer to a wire rack. Repeat to use all of the batter.

6 To serve, toast the crumpets on both sides and serve with butter.

Makes about 24

Scones

3 tbsp. butter, diced, plus extra
   to grease

1¾ cups plus 2 tbsp. self-rising flour, plus
   extra to dust

a pinch of salt

1 tsp. baking powder

about ½ cup (125ml) milk

beaten egg or milk to glaze

whipped cream, or butter and preserves
   to serve

TRY THIS

To guarantee a good rise, avoid
heavy handling and make sure the
rolled-out dough is at least ¾in.
(2cm) thick.

1 Heat the oven to 425°F (400°F for
convection ovens). Grease a baking
sheet. Sift the flour, salt, and baking
powder into a bowl. Cut in the butter
until the mixture resembles fine bread
crumbs. Using a knife to stir it in,
add enough milk to make a fairly
soft dough.

2 Gently roll or pat out the dough
on a lightly floured work surface to a
¾in. (2cm) thickness and then, using
a 2½in. (6cm) plain cutter, cut out
eight rounds.

3 Put on the baking sheet and brush the
tops with beaten egg or milk. Bake for
about 10 minutes until golden brown
and well risen. Transfer to a wire rack
to cool.

4 Serve warm, split and filled with
cream, or butter and preserves.

Makes 8

Cinnamon Whirls

Prep time: 20 minutes
Cooking time: 20 minutes, plus cooling

3 tbsp. superfine sugar, plus extra to dust the pan

13oz. (375g) ready-to-bake puff pastry dough in sheets, thawed if frozen

1 tsp. ground cinnamon

1 tsp. apple pie spice

1 egg, beaten

1 Heat the oven to 400°F (350°F for convection ovens). Sprinkle the work surface with sugar in a rectangle measuring 14 × 9in (35 × 22.5cm). Unroll the dough and lay it on top to fit the shape of the sugar rectangle. Trim the edges, then cut vertically down the middle to make two smaller rectangles.

2 Mix the cinnamon with the mixed spice and remaining sugar in a small bowl. Sprinkle half the spice mixture evenly over the dough rectangles. Fold the top and bottom edges of the dough pieces into the middle so they meet at the middle. Sprinkle the remaining spice mixture over the surface and repeat, folding the upper and lower folded edges in to meet in the middle. Finally, fold in half lengthwise to make a log shape.

3 Turn each roll over so the seam faces down, trim off the ragged ends, then cut into slices ½in. (1cm) wide. Lay the slices flat, spaced well apart, on two nonstick cookie sheets. Reshape them slightly if needed, but don't worry if the rolls look loose—as the dough bakes, they'll puff up.

4 Lightly brush each dough whirl with a little beaten egg, sprinkle with a dusting of sugar, and bake for 20 minutes, or until pale golden. Transfer to a wire rack to cool before serving.

Basic Baking Equipment

A selection of basic equipment is compulsory in order to bake successfully. Start with a few basic items and add to your collection as your skills increase (and as the demands of the recipes dictate).

Scales

Accurate measurement is essential when following most baking recipes. The electronic scale is the most accurate and can weigh up to 4½lb. (2kg) or 11lb. (5kg). Buy one with a flat platform on which you can put your bowl or measuring cup. Always set the scale to zero before adding the ingredients.

Measuring pitchers, cups, and spoons

Measuring pitchers can be plastic or glass, and are available, marked with both ounce and cup measurements.

Measuring cups are bought in sets of ¼ cup, ⅓ cup, ½ cup, and 1 cup. A standard 1 cup measure is equivalent to about 8oz. (240ml)

Measuring spoons are useful for the smallest units and accurate spoon measurements go up to 1 tbsp. (15ml). These can be plastic or metal and often come in sets attached together on a ring.

Mixing bowls

Stainless-steel bowls work best when you are using a hand-held mixer, or when you need to place the bowl into a larger bowl filled with ice water for chilling down, or to place it over simmering water (when melting chocolate, for example). Plastic or glass bowls are best if you need to use them in the microwave. Bowls with gently tapered sides—much wider at the rim than at the bottom—are useful for mixing dough.

Mixing spoons

For general mixing, a sturdy wooden spoon is ideal for working with thick mixtures, such as dough. In addition, a large metal spoon is invaluable for folding ingredients together.

Bakeware

As well as being thin enough to conduct heat quickly and efficiently, bakeware should be sturdy enough not to warp. Most bakeware is made from aluminum, and it can have an enamel or nonstick coatings.

A newer material for some bakeware is flexible, ovensafe silicone. Silicone is safe to handle straight from the oven, is inherently nonstick, and is also flexible—making it easy to remove muffins and other baked goods from their pans.

Baking trays/Baking sheets

Shallower than a roasting pan, these have many uses in baking. To avoid having to bake in batches, choose ones that are large, but which fit comfortably in your oven. Buy the best you can afford. Cookie sheets are flat.

Baking dishes

Are usually ceramic or Pyrex and you should have them in several sizes.

Cake pans

Available in many shapes and sizes, cake pans can be single-piece, loose-bottomed, or springform.

Loaf pans

Available in various sizes, but one of the most useful is a 9 x 5in. (22.5 x 12.5cm) standard loaf pan.

Pie pans

You should have both single-piece pans and loose-bottomed pans for flans and tarts.

Muffin pans

These come in various sizes and depths and are available in both aluminum and silicone. If you make a lot of muffins and cupcakes it's worth investing in different types.

Honey and Spice Loaf Cake

Prep time: 20 minutes
Cooking time: about 55 minutes, plus cooling and setting

2 tbsp. honey

1¾ sticks unsalted butter

heaped ⅓ cup packed dark soft brown
  sugar

2 extra-large eggs

1⅔ cups self-rising flour

1½ tsp. apple pie spice

1 cup confectioners' sugar, sifted

butter to serve (optional)

1　Put the honey, butter, and brown sugar into a pan and melt together over low heat. When the sugar has dissolved, turn up the heat until the mixture bubbles for 1 minute. Remove from the heat and cool for 15 minutes.

2　Heat the oven to 325°F (275°F for convection ovens). Line a 9 x 5in (22.5 x 12.5cm) loaf pan with baking parchment.

3　Mix the eggs into the melted butter. Sift the flour and mixed spice into a large bowl and add the butter mixture. Mix well, then pour into the prepared loaf pan.

4　Bake for 40–50 minutes until a skewer inserted into the middle comes out clean. Cool in the pan for 5 minutes, then turn out on to a wire rack (leave the lining paper on) and let cool completely. When the cake is cool, peel off the lining paper and put the cake on a serving plate.

5　To make the glaze, put the confectioners' sugar into a bowl and whisk in just enough water to get a runny consistency. Drizzle over the cake and let the glaze harden a little. Slice and serve with butter, if you like.

Cuts into 8 slices

Perfect Muffins

Muffins and cupcakes are members of the same family: individual cakes, usually based on a batter made with self-rising flour and baked in muffin pans so that they rise and set to an airy texture.

Banana and pecan muffins

To make 12 muffins, you will need: 2¼ cups self-rising flour, 1 tsp. baking soda, a pinch of salt, 3 very ripe, large peeled and mashed bananas, about 1lb. (450g), ½ cup plus 2 tbsp. sugar, 1 exrta-large egg, 5 tbsp. milk, 5 tbsp. melted butter, and ½ cup chopped roasted pecans.

1 Heat the oven to 350°F (300°F for convection ovens). Line a 12-hole muffin pan with paper cupcake cases. Sift together the flour, baking soda, and salt and set aside.

2 Combine the bananas, sugar, egg, and milk, then pour in the melted butter and mix well. Add to the flour mixture with the nuts, stirring quickly and gently with just a few strokes. Half-fill the muffin cups.

3 Bake for 20 minutes, or until golden and risen. Transfer to a wire rack and let cool.

TRY THIS

The secret to really light, fluffy muffins is a light hand, so be sure to sift the flour. Stir the mixture as little as possible; it's okay if it looks a little lumpy. Over-mixing will give you tough, chewy results.

Cheesy Spinach Muffins

Prep time: 15 minutes
Cooking time: 12–15 minutes

1½ cups baby spinach

1 cup plus 3 tbsp. self-rising flour

1 tsp. baking powder

2 tbsp. grated Parmesan-style cheese

heaped ½ cup finely chopped cheddar
   cheese,

2 tbsp. butter, melted

7 tbsp. milk

2 eggs

a small handful fresh parsley,
   finely chopped

salt and ground black pepper

1 Heat the oven to 400°F (350°F for convection ovens). Line six cups in a 12-hole muffin pan with paper cupcake cases. Put the spinach into a sieve and pour over boiling water until it wilts. Let the spinach cool, then squeeze out as much water as you can before finely chopping it. Set aside.

2 In a large bowl, mix together the flour, baking powder, most of the Parmesan and cheddar cheeses, and some seasoning.

3 In a separate bowl, whisk together the butter, milk, eggs, parsley, and chopped spinach. Quickly mix the wet ingredients into the dry. Don't worry if there are floury lumps, as these will bake out.

4 Divide the batter evenly between the paper cases, then sprinkle the remaining cheese over. Bake for 12–15 minutes until the muffins are golden and baked through. Serve warm.

SAVE TIME

Prepare the muffins to the end of step 2 up to one day in advance. Put the chopped spinach into a bowl, then cover and chill. Cover the flour and cheese mixture and chill, then complete the recipe to serve.

Makes 6

Honey and Yogurt Muffins

Prep time: 15 minutes
Cooking time: about 20 minutes, plus cooling

1¾ cups plus 2 tbsp. all-purpose flour

1½ tsp. baking powder

1 tsp. baking soda

½ tsp. each apple pie spice and
   ground nutmeg

a pinch of salt

heaped ½ cup ground oatmeal

⅓ cup unpacked light brown sugar

1 cup Greek-style yogurt

½ cup (125ml) milk

1 egg

4 tbsp. butter, melted and cooled

4 tbsp. honey

1 Heat the oven to 400°F (350°F for convection ovens). Line a 12-hole muffin pan with paper cupcake cases.

2 Sift the flour, baking powder, baking soda, apple pie spice, nutmeg, and salt into a bowl. Stir in the oatmeal and sugar.

3 Mix the yogurt with the milk in a bowl, then beat in the egg, butter, and honey. Pour onto the dry ingredients and stir in until just blended—don't overmix. Divide the batter between the paper cases.

4 Bake for 17–20 minutes until the muffins are well risen and just firm. Cool in the pan for 5 minutes, then transfer to a wire rack. Serve warm or cold. These are best eaten on the day they are made.

FREEZE AHEAD

To freeze ahead, complete the recipe, then cool, pack, seal, and freeze. Thaw at room temperature when ready to use.

Makes 12

Bran and Apple Muffins

Prep time: 20 minutes
Cooking time: 30 minutes, plus cooling

1 cup 2 percent milk

2 tbsp. orange juice

¾ cup All Bran

9 ready-to-eat dried prunes

scant ½ cup packed light brown sugar

2 egg whites

1 tbsp. Lyle's Golden Syrup

1 cup plus 3 tbsp. all-purpose flour, sifted

1 tsp. baking powder

1 tsp. ground cinnamon

1 eating apple, peeled and grated

raw or Turbinado sugar to sprinkle

1 Heat the oven to 375°F (325°F for convection ovens). Line a muffin pan with 10 paper cupcase cakes.

2 Mix the milk and orange juice with the All Bran in a bowl. Set aside for 10 minutes.

3 Put the prunes into a food processor or blender with 7 tbsp. water and blend for 2–3 minutes to make a puree, then add the brown sugar and blend briefly to mix.

4 Put the egg whites into a clean, greasefree bowl and whisk until soft peaks form. Add the whites to the milk mixture with the golden syrup, flour, baking powder, cinnamon, grated apple, and prune mixture. Fold all the ingredients together gently—don't overmix or the muffins will be tough.

5 Divide the batter among the paper cases and bake for 30 minutes, or until well risen and golden brown. Cool on a wire rack. Sprinkle with sugar just before serving. These are best eaten on the day they are made.

Makes 10

Blueberry Muffins

Prep time: 10 minutes
Cooking time: about 25 minutes, plus cooling

2 eggs

1 cup 2 percent milk

1¼ cups Turbinado sugar

2 tsp. vanilla extract

2¾ cups plus 1 tbsp. all-purpose flour

4 tsp. baking powder

1⅔ cups blueberries, frozen

finely grated zest of 2 lemons

HEALTHY TIP

Blueberries are bursting with health-boosting nutrients; they're rich in antioxidants, minerals, and vitamins A, B, C, and E.

1 Heat the oven to 400°F (350°F for convection ovens). Line a 12-hole muffin pan with paper cupcake cases.

2 Put the eggs, milk, sugar, and vanilla extract into a bowl and mix well.

3 Sift the flour and baking powder together into another bowl, then add the blueberries and lemon zest. Toss together and make a well in the middle.

4 Pour the egg mixture into the flour and blueberries and mix in gently—overbeating will make the muffins tough. Spoon the batter equally into the paper cases.

5 Bake for 20–25 minutes until risen and just firm. Transfer to a wire rack and let cool completely. These are best eaten on the day they are made.

Makes 12

Spiced Carrot Muffins

Prep time: 30 minutes
Cooking time: about 25 minutes, plus cooling

1 stick unsalted butter, softened

heaped ½ cup light brown sugar

3 pieces preserved ginger, drained and chopped

1 cup plus 3 tbsp. self-rising flour, sifted

1½ tsp. baking powder

1 tbsp. apple pie spice

¼ cup almond meal

3 eggs

finely grated zest of ½ orange

1½ cups peeled and grated carrots

½ cup chopped pecans

⅓ cup golden raisins

For the topping and decoration

¾ cup plus 2 tbsp. cream cheese

¾ cup confectioners' sugar

1 tsp. lemon juice

3 tbsp. white rum or orange liqueur (optional)

12 edible rose petals (optional)

1 Heat the oven to 350°F (325°F for convection ovens). Line a 12-hole muffin pan with paper cupcake cases.

2 Beat the butter, brown sugar and ginger together until pale and creamy. Add the flour, baking powder, spice, ground almonds, eggs, and orange zest, and beat well until combined. Stir in the carrots, pecans, and raisins. Divide the batter among the paper cases.

3 Bake for 20–25 minutes until risen and just firm. A skewer inserted into the middle of a muffin should come out clean. Transfer to a wire rack and leave to cool completely.

4 To make the topping, beat the cream cheese in a bowl until softened. Beat in the confectioners' sugar and lemon juice to make a smooth frosting that just holds its shape.

Makes 12

5 Drizzle each muffin with a little liqueur, if you like. Using a small knife, spread a little frosting over each muffin. Decorate with a rose petal, if you like.

Brown Sugar Muffins

Prep time: 10 minutes
Cooking time: about 35 minutes, plus cooling

12 brown sugar cubes

1 cup plus 3 tbsp. all-purpose flour

1½ tsp. baking powder

¼ tsp. salt

1 egg, beaten

⅓ cup superfine sugar

4 tbsp. unsalted butter, melted

½ tsp. vanilla extract

7 tbsp. milk

1 Heat the oven to 400°F (350°F for convection ovens). Line a muffin pan with six paper cupcake cases.

2 Roughly crush the sugar cubes and set aside. Sift together the flour, baking powder, and salt.

3 In a large bowl, combine the beaten egg, sugar, melted butter, vanilla extract, and milk.

4 Fold in the sifted flour and spoon the mixture into the muffin pan. Sprinkle with the brown sugar.

5 Bake for 30–35 minutes. Cool on a wire rack.

TRY THIS

Quickly transform this recipe into apple and cinnamon muffins: fold 5 tbsp. chunky applesauce and 1 tsp. ground cinnamon into the batter with the flour.

Makes 6

Good Eggs

Classic Omelet

TAKE 5

🍴 **Prep time:** 5 minutes
Cooking time: 5 minutes

2–3 eggs

1 tbsp. milk or water

2 tbsp. unsalted butter

salt and freshly ground black pepper

sliced or broiled tomatoes and freshly
    chopped flat leaf parsley to serve

1 Whisk the eggs in a bowl, just enough to break them down—overbeating spoils the texture of the omelet. Season and add the milk or water.

HEALTHY TIP

Eggs are a good protein source, with one egg providing about one-sixth of our daily requirement.

2 Heat the butter in an 7in. (17.5cm) omelet pan or nonstick skillet until it is foaming, but not brown. Add the eggs and stir gently with a fork or wooden spatula, gently scraping down the mixture from the sides to the middle as it sets, and letting the liquid egg in the middle run to the sides. When set, stop stirring and cook for 30 seconds or until the omelet is golden brown underneath and still creamy on top: don't overcook. If you are making a filled omelet, add the filling at this point.

3 Tilt the pan away from you slightly and use a spatula to fold over one-third of the omelet to the middle, then fold over the opposite third. Slide the omelet out onto a warm plate, letting it flip over so that the folded sides are underneath. Serve immediately, with tomatoes sprinkled with parsley.

Serves 1

Omelet Arnold Bennett

Prep time: 15 minutes
Cooking time: about 20 minutes

4oz. (125g) boneless smoked haddock

4 tbsp. butter

⅔ cup (150ml) heavy cream

3 eggs, separated

½ cup grated cheddar cheese

salt and freshly ground black pepper

arugula salad to serve

1 Put the fish in a pan and cover with water. Bring to a boil, reduce the heat, and simmer gently for 10 minutes. Drain and flake the fish, discarding the skin and bones.

2 Put the fish in a pan with half the butter and 2 tbsp. cream. Cook over high heat until the butter melts. Let cool.

3 Heat the broiler. Beat the egg yolks with 1 tbsp. cream and seasoning. Stir in the fish mixture. Put the egg whites into a clean, grease-free bowl and whisk until they form stiff peaks; fold into the yolks.

4 Heat the remaining butter in an omelet pan. Fry the egg mixture, but make sure it remains fairly fluid. Do not fold over. Slide it onto a flameproof serving dish.

5 Blend together the cheese and remaining cream, then spread it on top of the omelet and brown under the broiler. Serve immediately with an arugula salad.

Serves 2

Spanish Omelet

2lb. (900g) potatoes, peeled and left whole

3–4 tbsp. vegetable oil

1 onion, thinly sliced

8 eggs

3 tbsp. freshly chopped flat-leaf parsley

3 slices of bacon

salt and freshly ground black pepper

green salad to serve

1 Put the potatoes into a pot of cold salted water, then bring to a boil, reduce the heat, and simmer for 15–20 minutes until almost cooked. Drain. When the potatoes are cool enough to handle, slice them thickly.

2 Heat 1 tbsp. oil in an 7in. (17.5cm) nonstick skillet (suitable for use under the broiler). Add the onion and fry gently for 7–10 minutes until softened. Take the pan off the heat and set aside.

3 Lightly beat the eggs in a bowl and season well.

4 Heat the broiler. Heat the remaining oil in the skillet, then layer the potato slices, onion, and 2 tbsp. chopped parsley in the pan. Pour in the beaten eggs and cook for 5–10 minutes until the omelette is firm underneath. Meanwhile, fry the bacon until golden and crisp, and then break into pieces.

5 Put the omelet in the pan under the broiler for 2–3 minutes until the top is just set. Scatter the bacon and remaining chopped parsley over the surface. Serve wedges of the omelet with a green salad.

Eggs Benedict

Prep time: 15 minutes
Cooking time: 10 minutes

4 slices of bread

eggs

⅔ cup (150ml) bought hollandaise sauce

4 thin slices of lean ham

fresh parsley sprigs to garnish

1 Toast the bread. Poach the eggs. Gently warm the hollandaise sauce.
2 Top each slice of toast with a folded slice of ham, then with a poached egg. Finally, coat the eggs with hollandaise sauce.
3 Garnish each with a sprig of parsley and serve immediately.

TRY THIS

For a delicious alternative recipe try
Eggs Florentine:
Cook 2lb. (900g) washed spinach in a pot with a little salt until tender. Drain well, then chop and reheat with 1 tbsp. butter. Melt 2 tbsp. butter, stir in 3 tbsp. all-purpose flour, and cook, stirring, until thickened. Add ½ cup grated Gruyère or cheddar cheese and season. Do not let boil. Poach the eggs. Put the spinach into a baking dish, arrange the eggs on top, and pour the cheese sauce over them. Sprinkle with 2 tbsp. grated cheese and brown under the broiler.

Serves 4

Perfect Scrambled Eggs

There are numerous ways to cook with eggs—from the simplest techniques, such as boiling, to more complex techniques, such as making omelets, soufflés, and meringues. Follow these instructions for scrambled eggs with perfect results.

1. Allow 2 eggs per person. Break the eggs into a bowl, then beat well but lightly with a fork, and season with salt and freshly ground black pepper.

2. Melt 1 tsp. of butter in a small heavy-bottom pan over low heat—use a heat diffuser if you have one. (Using a nonstick pan minimizes the amount of butter you need to use.)

3. Pour in the eggs and start stirring immediately, using a wooden spatula or spoon to break up the lumps as they form. Keep the eggs moving around as much as possible during cooking.

4 As the eggs start to set, scrape the bottom of the pan to keep the eggs from overcooking and to break up any larger lumps that form. Your aim is to have a smooth mixture without any noticeable lumps.

5 Scrambled eggs can be well cooked and firm, or "loose" and runny; this is a matter of taste. They will continue to cook when taken off the heat, so remove them when they are still softer than you want to serve them.

TRY THIS

Microwave scrambled eggs
Put the eggs, milk, if you like, and the butter into a bowl and beat well. Microwave on full power for 1 minute (the mixture should be just starting to set around the edges), then beat again. Microwave again at full power for 2–3 minutes, stirring every 30 seconds, until the eggs are cooked the way you like them.

Scrambled Eggs with Smoked Salmon

Prep time: 10 minutes
Cooking time: 5 minutes

6 extra-large eggs

2 tbsp. butter, plus extra to spread

7 tbsp. mascarpone

4oz. (125g) smoked salmon, sliced, or smoked salmon trimmings

6 slices sourdough or rye bread, toasted, buttered, and cut into slim rectangles

salt and freshly ground black pepper

1 Crack the eggs into a bowl and lightly beat together. Season well.

2 Melt the butter in a nonstick pan over low heat. Add the eggs and stir constantly until the mixture thickens. Add the mascarpone and season well. Cook for 1–2 minutes longer until the mixture just becomes firm, then fold in the smoked salmon. Serve at once with hot toast.

Serves 4

Poached Eggs with Mushrooms

Prep time: 15 minutes
Cooking time: 20 minutes

8 Portobello mushrooms

2 tbsp. butter

8 eggs

3 cups baby spinach leaves

4 tsp. pesto sauce

1 Heat the oven to 400°F (350°F for convection ovens). Arrange the mushrooms in a single layer in a small roasting pan and dot with the butter. Roast for 15 minutes, or until golden brown and soft.

2 Meanwhile, bring a wide, shallow pan of water to a boil. When the mushrooms are half-cooked and the water is bubbling furiously, break the eggs into the pan, spaced well apart, then take the pan off the heat. The eggs will take about 6 minutes to cook.

3 When the mushrooms are tender, put them on a warm plate, cover, and put back into the turned-off oven to keep them warm.

4 Put the roasting pan over medium heat and add the spinach. Cook, stirring, for about 30 seconds until the spinach has just started to wilt.

5 The eggs should be set by now, so divide the mushrooms among four warm plates and top with a little spinach, a poached egg, and a teaspoonful of pesto.

HEALTHY TIP

Eggs once had a bad reputation, with many people who believed (wrongly) that they raised blood cholesterol levels. Scientists, however, have now found that most people can safely eat up to two eggs a day without any adverse effect on their cholesterol levels.

Baked Eggs

Prep time: 10 minutes
Cooking time: 15 minutes

2 tbsp. olive oil

1¾ cups chopped mushrooms

3 cups fresh spinach

2 eggs

2 tbsp. heavy cream

salt and freshly ground black pepper

HEALTHY TIP

Spinach is rich in iron, and is better absorbed when consumed with another vitamin C-rich food, such as orange juice, at the same meal.

1 Heat the oven to 400°F (350°F for convection ovens). Heat the oil in a large skillet. Add the mushrooms and stir-fry for 30 seconds. Add the spinach and stir-fry until wilted. Season to taste, then divide the mixture between two shallow baking dishes suitable for serving from.

2 Carefully break an egg into the middle of each dish, then spoon 1 tbsp. cream over it.

3 Bake for about 12 minutes until just set —the eggs will continue to bake a little once they're out of the oven. Grind a little more black pepper over the top, if you like, and serve.

Serves 2

Mixed Mushroom Frittata

Prep time: 15 minutes
Cooking time: about 20 minutes

1 tbsp. olive oil

4¼ cups sliced mixed mushrooms

2 tbsp. freshly chopped thyme

grated zest and juice of ½ lemon

1½ cups chopped watercress

6 eggs, beaten

salt and freshly ground black pepper

crisp green salad and wholegrain bread
    to serve

HEALTHY TIP

Eggs are a good source of protein—
2 eggs supply roughly one-third of
an adult's daily requirement—as
well as vitamins A and D.

1 Heat the oil in a large, deep skillet, suitable for use under the broiler, over a medium heat. Add the mushrooms and thyme and stir-fry for 4–5 minutes until the mixture starts to soften and brown. Stir in the lemon zest and juice and cook for 1 minute. Reduce the heat.

2 Heat the broiler. Add the watercress to the beaten eggs, season with salt and freshly ground black pepper, and pour into the pan. Cook on the hob for 7–8 minutes until the sides and base are firm but the middle is still a little soft.

3 Transfer to the broiler and cook for 4–5 minutes longer until just set. Cut the frittata into wedges and serve with a crisp green salad and chunks of wholegrain bread.

Serves 4

Perfect Eggs

Follow these tried-and-tested steps for poached, coddled, and boiled eggs.

Poaching

1 Heat about 3¼in. (8cm) of lightly salted water in a shallow skillet to a bare simmer. Crack a very fresh egg into a cup, then slip it into the water. (The whites in a fresh egg are firmer and will form a "nest" for the yolk, while older egg whites are watery and spread out in the pan.)
2 Cook for 3–4 minutes until the white is barely set. Remove the egg with a slotted spoon and drain on paper towels.

Perfect coddling

1 Using a slotted spoon, gently lower whole eggs into a pot of simmering water, then take the pot off the heat.
2 Let the eggs stand in the water for 4–5 minutes, where they will cook gently with the residual heat of the water.

2

Perfect boiled eggs

There are two ways to boil an egg: starting in boiling water or starting in cold water. Both work well, as long as you follow certain rules:

❑ The egg must be at room temperature before you start

❑ For both methods, cover the eggs with water, plus 1in. (2.5cm) or so extra

❑ If starting in boiling water, use a needle, if you like, to pierce the broad end of the shell. This allows air in the pocket at the base of the egg to escape and avoids cracking

❑ Gently lower the eggs into the water using a long-handled spoon to avoid cracking them

❑ Cook at a simmer rather than a rolling boil

Boiling: method 1

1 Bring a small pot of water to a boil. Once the water is boiling, add an egg. For a soft-boiled egg, cook for 6 minutes; for a salad egg, cook for 8 minutes; and for a hard-boiled egg, cook for 10 minutes.

2 Remove the egg from the water with a slotted spoon and serve.

Boiling: method 2

1 Put a medium egg in a small pot and cover with cold water. Cover and bring to a boil. When the water begins to boil, uncover and cook for 2 minutes for a soft-boiled egg, 5 minutes for a salad egg, and 7 minutes for a hard-boiled egg.

Duck Egg and Asparagus Dippers

Prep time: 15 minutes
Cooking time: about 6 minutes

1lb. 5oz. (600g) asparagus spears
6 duck eggs
extra virgin olive oil, to drizzle
salt and freshly ground black pepper
sourdough bread (optional) to serve

1 Holding both ends of an asparagus spear in your hands, bend gently until it snaps. Discard the woody end (or keep to make soups or stocks). Trim all the remaining spears to this length. Use a vegetable peeler to shave any knobbly or woody pieces below the tip of each spear.

2 Divide the asparagus equally into six piles, then tie each neatly into a bundle with string.

3 Bring two medium pots of water to a boil. Add the eggs to one pot and simmer for exactly 5½ minutes. Add the asparagus bundles to the other pot and cook for 1 minute, or until just tender. Drain the asparagus and let it steam-dry in the colander for 3 minutes. Drain the eggs.

4 Put one asparagus bundle on each plate, drizzle with a little extra virgin olive oil and season with salt and ground black pepper. Serve with the eggs, plus a slice of sourdough bread, if you like.

SAVE TIME

Prepare the asparagus to the end of step 2 up to 2 hours in advance. Chill the bundles, then complete the recipe to serve.

Huevos Rancheros

Prep time: 10 minutes
Cooking time: about 15 minutes

1 tbsp. vegetable oil

1 red onion, thinly sliced

1 each yellow and red bell pepper,
   seeded and thinly sliced

1 red chili pepper, seeded and thinly
   sliced

2 cans (15-oz./425g) crushed tomatoes

½ tsp. Italian seasoning

4 extra-large eggs

small handful flat-leaf parsley,
   roughly chopped

crusty bread, to serve

1 Heat the oil in a large skillet over high heat. Fry the onion, peppers, and chili pepper for 3 minutes, or until just softened. Add the tomatoes and Italian seasoning. Season and simmer for 3 minutes.

2 Break an egg into a small cup. Use a wooden spoon to scrape an indentation in the tomato mixture, then quickly drop in the egg. Repeat with the remaining eggs, spacing evenly around the tomato mixture. Cover and simmer for 3-5 minutes until the eggs are just set. Sprinkle with parsley and serve with plenty of crusty bread.

Serves 6

Sweet Plates

Perfect Batters

Batters can serve a number of purposes, and are remarkably versatile for something so simple. All you need to remember when working with them is to mix quickly and lightly.

Crepes

To make eight crepes, you will need:
1 cup all-purpose flour, a pinch of salt,
1 egg, 1¼ cups (300ml) milk, oil, and
butter to fry.

1   Sift the flour and salt into a bowl,
    make a well in the middle and
    whisk in the egg. Gradually beat in
    the milk to make a smooth batter,
    then let it stand for 20 minutes.
2   Heat a little butter in a heavy-
    bottomed skillet to coat it. Pour
    in a little batter and tilt the pan to
    coat the bottom thinly and evenly.
3   Cook over medium-high heat for
    1 minute, or until golden. Turn
    over carefully and cook the other
    side for 30 seconds to 1 minute.

Drop Scones

For 15–18 pancakes, you will need:
1 cup self-rising flour, 2 tbsp. sugar,
1 beaten egg, ⅔ cup (150ml) milk, and
a little vegetable oil to grease.

1   Mix the flour and sugar in a bowl.
    Make a well in the middle and
    mix in the egg and a little milk
    to achieve the consistency of
    thick cream.
2   Oil a griddle or heavy skillet and
    heat it until medium-hot. Drop
    some of the batter in small rounds
    onto the griddle or pan and cook
    over steady heat until bubbles rise
    to the surface—2–3 minutes.
3   Turn and cook for 2–3 minutes
    longer, then remove to a clean
    dish towel. Cover with another
    dish towel to keep them moist, and
    continue cooking the scones until
    you have used all the batter.

2

3

Lemon and Blueberry Pancakes

Prep time: 15 minutes
Cooking time: about 15 minutes

1 cup wholewheat flour

1 tsp. baking powder

¼ tsp. baking soda

2 tbsp. sugar

finely grated zest of 1 lemon

½ cup plain yogurt

2 tbsp. milk

2 eggs

3 tbsp. butter

⅔ cup blueberries

1 tsp. sunflower oil

plain yogurt and fruit compote (or preserves) to serve

1 Sift the flour, baking powder, and baking soda into a bowl. Add the sugar and lemon zest. Pour in the yogurt and milk. Break the eggs into the mixture and whisk together.

2 Melt 2 tbsp. butter in a pan, add to the bowl with the blueberries and stir everything together.

3 Heat a dot of the remaining butter with the oil in a skillet over medium heat until hot. Add four large spoonfuls of the mixture to the pan to make four pancakes. After about 2 minutes, flip them over and cook for 1–2 minutes longer. Repeat with the remaining mixture, adding a dot more butter each time.

4 Serve with plain yogurt and some fruit compote or preserves.

TRY THIS

Instead of fresh blueberries and lemon, use ⅔ cup chopped ready-to-eat dried apricots and 2 tsp. grated fresh ginger.

Classic Pancakes

Prep time: 10 minutes, plus standing
Cooking time: about 15 minutes

1½ cups less 2 tbsp. self-rising flour

1 tsp. baking powder

1 tsp. baking soda

a pinch of salt

¼ cup superfine sugar

1 extra-large egg, beaten

1¼ cups (300ml) buttermilk

4 tbsp. butter, melted and cooled slightly, plus extra for frying

milk (optional)

crispy fried bacon and maple syrup to serve

1 In a bowl, sift together the flour, baking powder, and baking soda with a pinch of salt. Stir in the sugar.

2 Combine the egg, buttermilk, and butter, then gradually whisk into the flour to make a smooth batter—it should be the consistency of heavy cream, so add a drop of milk if necessary. Let the mixture stand for 5 minutes.

3 Put a large skillet over medium heat until hot. Brush the surface with a little melted butter. Pour about 2 tbsp. of the batter into the pan to form a 4in. (10cm) circle—the batter should spread naturally to that size if it is the right consistency. Cook for 2 minutes, or until small holes appear on the surface, then turn over and cook for 1–2 minutes longer. Do this in batches, depending on the size of your pan, and regrease the bottom when necessary. Serve warm with plenty of crispy bacon and maple syrup.

Makes 12

Cinnamon Crepes

Prep time: 5 minutes, plus standing
Cooking time: 20 minutes

1 cup plus 3 tbsp. all-purpose flour

½ tsp. ground cinnamon

1 egg

1¼ cups (300ml) 2 percent milk

olive oil to fry

fruit compote or preserves, or sugar, and
Greek-style yogurt to serve

SAVE MONEY

If you don't have any fruit compote,
preserves, or yogurt, try serving
the crepes with sliced bananas and
vanilla ice cream instead.

1 Whisk the flour, cinnamon, egg and milk together in a large bowl to make a smooth batter. Let it rest for 20 minutes.

2 Heat a heavy-bottomed skillet over medium heat. When the pan is really hot, add 1 tsp. oil, pour in a ladleful of batter, and tilt the pan to coat the bottom with an even layer. Cook for 1 minute, or until golden. Flip over and cook for 1 minute. Repeat with the remaining batter, adding extra oil if necessary, to make more pancakes. Serve with a fruit compote, preserves, or a sprinkling of sugar, and a dollop of yogurt.

Scotch Pancakes

Prep time: 10 minutes
Cooking time: about 18 minutes

1 cup self-rising flour

2 tbsp. sugar

1 egg, beaten

⅔ cup (150ml) milk

vegetable oil to grease

whipped cream and jam, or butter,
    to serve

1 Mix the flour and sugar together in a bowl. Make a well in the middle and mix in the egg, with enough of the milk to make a batter the consistency of heavy cream—working as quickly and lightly as possible.

2 Cook the mixture in batches: drop spoonfuls onto an greased hot griddle or heavy-bottomed skillet. Keep the griddle at a steady heat and when bubbles rise to the surface of the pancake and burst, after 2–3 minutes, turn over with a metal spatula.

3 Cook for 2–3 minutes longer until golden brown on the other side.

4 Put the cooked pancakes on a clean dish towel and cover with another dish towel to keep them moist. Serve warm, with whipped cream and jam, or butter.

Makes 15–18

Crepes Suzette

Prep time: 20 minutes, plus standing
Cooking time: 15 minutes

1 quantity crepe batter (see page 92)

1 tsp. confectioners' sugar

grated zest of ½ orange

1 tsp. butter, plus extra to fry

2 tbsp. brandy

For the orange sauce

¼ cup sugar

4 tbsp. butter

juice of 2 oranges

grated zest of 1 lemon

3 tbsp. Cointreau

1 Flavor the crepe batter with the confectioners' sugar and orange zest, then let it rest for 30 minutes. Just before cooking the crepes, melt 1 tsp. of butter and stir it into the batter.

2 To cook the crepes, heat 1 tsp. of butter in a 6–7in. (15–17.5cm) heavy-bottomed skillet. Pour in just enough batter to cover the bottom, swirling it to coat. Cook over medium heat for about 1 minute until the crepe is golden underneath. Using a metal spatula, flip it over and cook briefly on the other side. Lift onto a plate, cover with parchment paper, and keep warm while you cook the others in the same way, using more butter for frying if required, interleaving each with paper to keep separate.

3 To make the orange sauce, put the sugar into a large, heavy-bottomed skillet and heat slowly, shaking the pan occasionally, until the sugar has dissolved and turned golden brown. Remove from the heat and add the butter, orange juice, and lemon zest. Put the pan back onto the heat, and stir the sauce until it begins to simmer. Add the Cointreau.

4 Fold each crepe in half and then in half again. Put all the crepes back into the pan and simmer for a few minutes to reheat, spooning the sauce over them.

5 To flambé, warm the brandy and pour it over the crepes. Using a long-reach match and standing well clear, ignite the brandy. When the flame dies down, serve the crepes immediately.

Serves 4

Waffles

Prep time: 5 minutes
Cooking time: 16 minutes

1 cup self-rising flour

a pinch of salt

1 tbsp. sugar

1 egg, separated

2 tbsp. butter, melted

⅔ cup (150ml) milk

½ tsp. vanilla extract (optional)

butter and maple syrup to serve

1 Heat your waffle iron.

2 Mix the flour, salt, and sugar together in a bowl. Add the egg yolk, melted butter, milk, and vanilla, if you like, and whisk together.

3 Put the egg white into a clean, grease-free bowl and whisk until it forms stiff peaks; fold into the batter. Pour just enough batter onto the iron to run over the surface.

4 Close the iron and cook for 2–3 minutes, turning the iron if using a nonelectric type. When the waffle is cooked, it should be golden brown and crisp and come away easily from the iron—if it sticks, cook for a minute longer. Cook the remaining batter in the same way.

5 Serve immediately with butter and maple syrup. Alternatively, layer the waffles with whipped cream or vanilla ice cream and fresh fruit.

Serves 4

French Toast

2 eggs

⅔ cup (150ml) 2 percent milk

a generous pinch of freshly grated nutmeg or ground cinnamon

4 slices white bread, or raisin bread, crusts removed, and each slice cut into four rectangles

4 tbsp. butter

vegetable oil for frying

1 tbsp. sugar

1. Put the eggs, milk, and nutmeg or cinnamon into a shallow dish and beat together.
2. Dip the pieces of bread into the mixture, coating them well.
3. Melt half the butter with 1 tbsp. oil in a heavy-based skillet. When the butter is foaming, fry the egg-coated pieces of bread in batches until golden on both sides, adding more butter and oil as needed. Sprinkle with sugar and serve.

SAVE MONEY

Use leftover bread for this tasty brunch or breakfast favorite. Serve with bacon and maple syrup.

Serves 4

Orange French Toast

2 extra-large eggs

⅔ cup (150ml) milk

finely grated zest of 1 orange

4 tbsp. butter

8 slices of raisin bread,
   halved diagonally

1 tbsp. confectioners' sugar

vanilla ice cream and orange segments
   to serve (optional)

1 Lightly whisk the eggs, milk, and orange zest together in a bowl.

2 Heat the butter in a large skillet over medium heat. Dip the slices of raisin bread into the egg mixture, then fry on both sides until golden.

3 Sprinkle the bread with the sugar and serve immediately with ice cream and orange slices, if you like.

Sandwiches
and Savories

Oatmeal Soda Bread

Prep time: 15 minutes
Cooking time: 25 minutes, plus cooling

2 tbsp. butter, plus extra to grease

2¼ cups wholewheat flour

scant 1 cup steel-cut oats

2 tsp. cream of tartar

1 tsp. salt

about 1¼ cups (300ml) milk and water, mixed

butter to serve

1 Heat the oven to 425°F (400°F for convection ovens). Grease a 9 x 5in. (22.5 x 12.5cm) loaf pan and line with parchment paper.

2 Mix together all the dry ingredients in a bowl. Cut in the butter.

3 Add the milk and water to make a soft dough. Spoon into the prepared loaf pan.

4 Bake for 25 minutes, or until golden brown and well risen. Turn out and cool on a wire rack. Serve with butter. This is best eaten on the day it is made.

HEALTHY TIP

This bread contains oats, which are rich in betaglucan, a soluble fiber that helps lower levels of cholesterol in the bloodstream. It also helps make you feel full longer and control blood sugar levels. Oats are also a good source of B vitamins and vitamin E.

Makes 1 loaf—cuts into about 10 slices

White Farmhouse Loaf

Bread Machine Recipe

Prep time: 10 minutes, plus kneading
Cooking time: as per your machine, plus cooling

4 cups all-purpose flour, plus extra
   to sprinkle

1 tbsp. sugar

2 tbsp. powdered milk

1½ tsp. salt

2 tbsp. butter

1 tsp. active dry yeast

1 Put the ingredients, including 1¾ cups (350ml) water, into the bread machine bowl and follow the manufacturer's directions.

2 Fit the bucket into the bread-maker and set to the basic program with a crust of your choice. Press "Start."

3 Just before baking begins, brush the top of the dough with water and sprinkle with flour. If preferred, slash the top of the bread lengthwise with a sharp knife, taking care not to scratch the bucket.

4 After baking, remove the bucket from the machine, then turn out the loaf onto a wire rack to cool.

Makes 1 loaf—cuts into about 12 slices

Dos and don'ts of breadmaking

1 Make sure shaped dough has risen sufficiently—usually to double.

2 Always oil or flour the loaf pan, or cookie sheet, to prevent sticking.

3 Make sure the oven is at the correct temperature before you begin baking.

4 Bake on a heated ceramic baking stone if possible, even if the bread is in a loaf pan. The heat of the stone will give the bread a crisp base.

5 If baked bread is left for too long either in the loaf pan or on the cookie sheet, steam will gather and, as a result, the underneath will start to become soggy. To prevent this, always remove the loaf immediately and put it on a wire rack, then let it cool completely before slicing.

Dos and don'ts of machine-baked bread

1 Use recipes that have been designed for bread machine use only, because conventional bread recipes use different quantities of ingredients and are not converted easily.

2 Measure out all the ingredients carefully, because exact quantities are essential for a perfect loaf.

3 Always follow the bread-machine directions closely; it is essential that the ingredients go into the machine in the order stated, because the yeast must not come into contact with the liquid until the machine begins to mix.

4 Avoid lifting the lid during the rising and baking cycles, because this can cause the loaf to sink.

5 The loaf is best removed from the machine as soon as it is baked, otherwise it will become soggy.

Herby Mushrooms on Toast

Prep time: 20 minutes
Cooking time: about 20 minutes

4 extra-large eggs

2 tbsp. butter

4 shallots, finely diced

3 garlic cloves, crushed

8½ cups chopped cremini mushrooms

2 tbsp. marsala or sherry, optional

2 tbsp. each chopped fresh tarragon
   and parsley

4 sourdough bread slices, freshly toasted

mixed green salad, to serve

1 Start by bringing a pot of water to a boil. Crack an egg into a cup or ramekin. Swirl the boiling water, then tip in the egg. Quickly crack another egg and add it to the water. Simmer for 3–4 minutes until the egg whites are set and the yolk remains soft. (To check, lift the egg out and gently prod it with your finger.) Transfer the cooked eggs to a shallow dish of warm water. Repeat with the remaining eggs.

2 Melt the butter in a large skillet. Add the shallots and garlic and cook for 10 minutes. Turn up the heat, add the mushrooms, and sauté for 5 minutes. Add the marsala or sherry, if using, then stir in the herbs. Check the seasoning.

3 Top each piece of toast with a pile of mushrooms. Lift the eggs out of the water and dab dry with a paper towel. Put an egg on each slice of toast and serve with a green salad.

Serves 4

Mozzarella Mushrooms

Prep time: about 3 minutes
Cooking time: about 20 minutes

8 large portabella mushrooms

8 slices marinated red bell pepper

8 fresh basil leaves

5oz. (150g) mozzarella cheese,
   cut into 8 slices

4 English muffins, halved

salt and freshly ground black pepper

green salad to serve

HEALTHY TIP

Mushrooms are an excellent source of potassium—a mineral that helps lower elevated blood pressure and reduces the risk of stroke. One medium portabella mushroom has even more potassium than a banana or a glass of orange juice. Mushrooms contain antioxidant nutrients that help inhibit the development of cancers of the breast and prostate.

1 Heat the oven to 400°F (350°F for convection ovens). Lay the mushrooms side by side in a roasting pan and season with salt and ground black pepper. Top each mushroom with a slice of red pepper and a basil leaf. Lay a slice of mozzarella on top of each mushroom and season again.

2 Roast for 15–20 minutes until the mushrooms are tender and the cheese has melted.

3 Meanwhile, toast the muffin halves until golden. Put a mozzarella mushroom on top of each muffin half. Serve immediately with a green salad.

Serves 4

Low-GI Beans on Toast

Prep time: 5 minutes
Cooking time: 10 minutes

1 tbsp. olive oil

2 garlic cloves, thinly sliced

1 can (15-oz./425g) cannellini beans, drained and rinsed

1 can (15-oz./425g) chickpeas, drained and rinsed

1 can (15-oz./425g) crushed tomatoes

2 fresh rosemary sprigs

4 slices of sourdough or wholewheat bread

¼ cup freshly grated Parmesan cheese

1 Heat the oil in a pan over low heat. Add the garlic and cook for 1 minute, stirring gently.

2 Add the beans and chickpeas to the pan with the tomatoes, then bring to a boil. Strip the leaves from the rosemary sprigs, then chop finely and add to the pan. Reduce the heat and simmer for 8–10 minutes until thickened.

3 Meanwhile, toast the bread. Grate the Parmesan into the bean mixture, andstir once, then spoon it over the toast and serve immediately.

Serves 4

Traditional Kippers

Prep time: about 5 minutes
Cooking time: about 15 minutes

2 kippers

butter, freshly chopped parsley, and
toast to serve

1 Cook the kippers using one of the
following methods: broil the kippers
for 5 minutes or so; or put them in a
pot of boiling water and leave them
in a warm place for 5–10 minutes;
alternatively, wrap them in foil and
cook them in an oven heated to
375°F (325°F for convection ovens)
for 10–15 minutes.

2 Serve with butter, parsley, and toast.

Smoked Haddock Kedgeree

Prep time: 30 minutes, plus chilling (optional)
Cooking time: about 15 minutes

¾ cup long-grain rice

1lb. (450g) smoked haddock fillets

2 eggs, hard-boiled and shelled

6 tbsp. butter

salt and cayenne pepper

freshly chopped parsley to garnish

1 Cook the rice in a pot of fast-boiling salted water until tender. Drain well and rinse under cold water.

2 Meanwhile, put the haddock in a large skillet with just enough water to cover. Bring to simmering point, then simmer for 10–15 minutes until tender. Drain, skin, and flake the fish, discarding the bones.

3 Chop one egg and slice the other into rings. Melt the butter in a pan, add the cooked rice, fish, chopped egg, salt, and cayenne pepper. Stir over medium heat for 5 minutes, or until hot. Pile the mixture onto a warm serving dish and garnish with parsley and the sliced egg.

Serves 4

Welsh Rarebit

Prep time: 15 minutes
Cooking time: about 15 minutes

1 can (15-oz./425g) crushed tomatoes

½ tbsp. tomato paste

1 small shallot, finely sliced

1½ cups grated aged cheddar cheese

½ tsp. Dijon mustard

4 tbsp. ale or beer

few dashes Worcestershire sauce

1 extra-large egg yolk

1½ tbsp. finely chopped fresh parsley

8 crumpets

salt and freshly ground black pepper

crisp green salad to serve

1 Put the canned tomatoes, tomato paste, and shallot into a small pot. Bring to a boil, then reduce the heat and simmer for 10 minutes. Check the seasoning.

2 Meanwhile, mix the cheese, mustard, ale, Worcestershire sauce, egg yolk, parsley, and seasoning together in a bowl.

3 Heat the broiler. Arrange the crumpets on a baking sheet and toast until golden. Divide and spread the tomato sauce equally over the toasted crumpets, then top each with an equal amount of the cheese mixture. Broil for 3–5 minutes until bubbling and golden. Serve with a crisp green salad.

Serves 4

BLT-Topped Bagels with Hollandaise Sauce

Prep time: 15 minutes
Cooking time: 8 minutes

3 large bagels, cut in half horizontally

2 tbsp. butter, softened

12 slices of bacon

2 tsp. olive oil

3 tomatoes, cut into thick slices

⅔ cup (150ml) bought hollandaise sauce

3oz. (75g) arugula

freshly ground black pepper

1 Toast the halved bagels under the broiler until golden. Spread generously with the butter. Cover the bagels with a piece of foil and keep them warm. Meanwhile, fry the bacon until crisp, then keep warm.

2 Heat the oil in a small skillet until very hot. Add the tomatoes and fry for about 1 minute until lightly charred. Put the hollandaise sauce in a small pan and heat gently.

3 To assemble, top the warm bagels with a few arugula leaves, the tomatoes and bacon. Spoon the warm hollandaise sauce over the bacon and season with pepper. Serve immediately.

Serves 6

Croque Monsieur

Prep time: 5 minutes
Cooking time: 8 minutes

4 slices of white bread

butter, softened, to spread, plus extra for frying

Dijon mustard, to taste

4oz. (125g) Gruyère cheese

4 slices of cooked ham

1 Spread each slice of bread on both sides with the butter. Then spread one side of two slices of bread with a little Dijon mustard.

2 Divide the cheese and ham between the two bread slices with mustard. Top each with the remaining bread and press down.

3 Heat a griddle or frying pan with a little butter until hot. Add the sandwiches and fry for 2–3 minutes on each side until golden and crispy, and the cheese starts to melt. Slice in half and serve immediately.

Serves 2

Smoothies and Drinks

Perfect Smoothies and Purees

Fruit, whether cooked or raw, can be transformed into a smooth drink or sauce by pureeing. Smoothies make a healthy breakfast or snack that is bursting with flavor.

Making smoothies

To serve four, you will need:
4 passion fruit, ⅔ cup (150ml) low-fat yogurt, 4 bananas, a small bunch of grapes.

1. Halve the passion fruit and scoop the pulp into a blender. Add the remaining ingredients. Crush 8 ice cubes and add to the blender.
2. Process until smooth and pour into glasses. Serve immediately.

Pureeing in a blender

Some fruit can be pureed raw,
while others are better cooked.
Wait for cooked fruit to cool before
processing it.

1 Blend a spoonful of fruit until
   smooth, then add another
   spoonful and blend. Add rest
   of fruit in batches.
2 For a very smooth puree, pass
   through a fine sieve.

Banana Vitality Shake

Prep time: 10 minutes

2 tbsp. whole shelled almonds

1 large ripe banana

⅔ cup (150ml) low-fat milk

⅔ cup (150ml) low-fat plain yogurt

2 tsp. powdered egg white

2 tsp. wheat germ

1–2 tsp. maple syrup

a pinch of freshly grated nutmeg

1 Grind the almonds in a spice grinder or food processor—the mixture needs to be very fine to blend well.

2 Peel and roughly chop the banana, then put into a blender with the ground almonds. Add the milk, yogurt, powdered egg white, and wheat germ to the blender and blend for a few seconds until smooth.

3 Add maple syrup to taste, then pour into two glasses and serve immediately, sprinkled with nutmeg.

HEALTHY TIP

A good source of protein, calcium, carbohydrates, and B vitamins, this shake makes a highly nutritious supplement for regular exercisers. Almonds add healthy monounsaturated fats, as well as vitamin E and iron.

Serves 2—makes about 2½ cups (600ml)

Creamy Dairy-Free Banana

TAKE 5

🍴 **Prep time:** 5 minutes

1 large ripe banana

4oz. (125g) silken tofu, well chilled

¾ cup unsweetened soy milk,
   well chilled

2 tsp. thick honey

a few drops of vanilla extract

1 Peel the banana and slice thickly.
   Put into a blender.

2 Drain the tofu and mash lightly with
   a fork, then add to the blender.

3 Pour in the milk and add the honey
   with a few drops of vanilla extract.
   Blend for a few seconds until thick
   and smooth. Pour the smoothie into
   a large glass and serve.

TRY THIS

Silken tofu is very smooth and
is the best for blending in drinks.
Firmer types can be used, but give
a grainier texture when blended.

Serves 1, makes about 1½ cups (400ml)

Breakfast Smoothie

TAKE
5

🍴 **Prep time:** 5 minutes

¾ cup plus 2 tbsp. percent milk

¾ cup plus 2 tbsp. plain yogurt

scant 1 cup mix of frozen berries—
we used a mix of blackberries,
blueberries, and black currants

2 tbsp. rolled oats

2 tbsp. honey

1 Put all the ingredients into a blender
and blend until smooth. Pour into two
tall glasses and serve.

SAVE TIME

If you prefer to have your breakfast
ready to go, make a double batch
of smoothies in the evening, then
transfer the mixture to another
container and chill for up to two
days. Simply stir before serving.

Serves 2

Perfect Smoothie Boosts

There are many ingredients that you can add to smoothies if you have specific nutritional requirements.

Acidophilus

A probiotic: "friendly" bacteria that promotes good health. Acidophilus is most beneficial when taken if you are suffering from diarrhea or after a course of antibiotics, or if you have digestive problems, such as irritable bowel syndrome (IBS). Available from most pharmacies and health food stores in capsule form, which usually need to be kept in the refrigerator. Probiotics are now included in some bought health drinks and yogurt products.

Bee Pollen

See page 148 for details and advice on where you can buy bee pollen.

Brewers' yeast

A by-product of beer brewing, brewers' yeast is exceptionally rich in B vitamins, with high levels of iron, zinc, magnesium, and potassium. Highly concentrated and an excellent pick-me-up, but the flavor is strong and needs to be mixed with other ingredients. Available as pills or powder.

Warning: brewer's yeast is high in purines, so it should be avoided by gout sufferers.

Echinacea

Echinacea, a native plant of North America, is taken to support a healthy immune system and has antiviral and antibacterial properties. Comes in capsules and in extracts taken as drops, so is easy to add to smoothies.

Warning: not recommended for use during pregnancy or when breastfeeding.

Eggs
Although they are high in protein, eggs also contain cholesterol, so you might need to limit your intake (ask your doctor). Egg white powder is low in fat and can be added to smoothies for a protein boost. Always use the freshest eggs for smoothies.
Warning: raw egg should not be eaten by the elderly, children, babies, pregnant women, or those with an impaired immune system, because there can be a risk of contracting salmonella.

Ginseng
Derived from the roots of a plant grown in Russia, Korea, and China. The active constituents are ginsenosides, reputed to stimulate the hormones and increase energy. Available in root form for grinding or powdered.
Warning: should not be taken by those suffering from hypertension.

Nuts
Packed with nutrients, nuts are a concentrated form of protein and are rich in antioxidants, vitamins B1, B6, and E, and many minerals. Brazil nuts are one of the best sources of selenium in the diet. Nuts do have a high fat content, however, but it is mostly unsaturated fat. Walnuts are particularly high in omega-3, an essential fatty acid that is needed for healthy heart and brain function. Brazil, cashew, coconut, peanut, and macadamia nuts contain more saturated fat, so should be used sparingly. Almonds are particularly easy to digest. Finely chop or grind the nuts just before using for maximum freshness.

Seeds

Highly nutritious, seeds contain a good supply of essential fatty acids (EFAs). Flaxseed (linseed) is particularly beneficial, as it is one of the richest sources of omega-3 EFAs, with 57 percent more than oily fish. Pumpkin, sesame, and sunflower seeds also work well in smoothies. They are best bought in small amounts—their fat content makes them go rancid quickly, so store in airtight containers in the refrigerator. Grind them just before use for maximum benefit, or use the oils, which have to be stored in the refrigerator.

Sprouting seeds

These are simply seeds from a variety of plants, such as sunflower, chickpea, and mung bean, which have been given a little water and warmth and have started to grow. Sprouts are full of vitamins, minerals, proteins, and carbohydrates. They are relatively soft so they blend easily into savory smoothies.

Oats

Sold in the form of wholegrain, rolled, flaked, or ground oats are high in protein, vitamin B complex, vitamin E, potassium, calcium, phosphorus, iron, and zinc; they are easy to digest and can soothe the digestive tract. They are also a rich source of soluble fiber, which helps to lower high blood cholesterol levels, which, in turn, helps reduce the risk of heart disease. Toasted oatmeal has a nutty flavor and is ideal for smoothies.

Warning: oats should be avoided by those on a gluten-free diet, unless they are labelled "gluten-free."

Wheat bran and germ

Wheat bran is the outside of the wheat grain removed during milling; it is very high in fiber and adds bulk to the diet. It is bland in taste, but adds a crunchy texture. Wheat germ, from the middle of the grain, is very nutritious and easy to digest, with a mild flavor. Highly perishable, store in the refrigerator once the container is opened.

Warning: keep your intake of bran to moderate levels; large amounts can prevent vitamins and minerals from being absorbed.

Nondairy alternatives

Soy milk and yogurt

If you are allergic to dairy products or lactose-intolerant, drinking milk can cause a variety of symptoms, including skin rashes and eczema, asthma, and irritable bowel syndrome. Soy milk and yogurt are useful alternatives—look for calcium-enriched products. Good nondairy sources of calcium suitable for adding to smoothies include dark green leafy vegetables, such as watercress and spinach, and apricots.

Silken tofu

This protein-rich, dairy-free product adds a creamy texture to fruit and vegetable smoothies.

Busy Bee's Comforter

Prep time: 5 minutes

---

2 lemons

⅔ cup (150ml) full-fat plain or soy
   yogurt, at room temperature

1–2 tsp. thick honey

2–3 tsp. bee pollen or equivalent
   in capsule form

1 Using a sharp knife, cut off the peel
  from one lemon, removing as much of
  the white pith as possible. Chop the
  flesh roughly, discarding any seeds,
  and put into a blender. Squeeze the
  juice from the remaining lemon and
  add to the blender.

2 Spoon in the yogurt and blend until
  smooth. Taste and sweeten with honey
  as necessary. Stir in the bee pollen,
  then pour into a glass and serve
  immediately.

HEALTHY TIP

You can buy bee pollen at health
food stores and online. This drink
is a very good source of protein
and calcium. It contains honey,
which is a source of slow-releasing
sugars, and a powerful antibacterial
and antiviral ingredient. Note, this
drink is unsuitable for those with
an allergy to pollen, such as
hayfever sufferers.

Serves 1, makes about ¾ cup (175ml)

Apricot and Orange Smoothie

Prep time: 5 minutes, plus chilling

1 can (15-oz./425g) apricots in
   natural juice

⅔ cup (150g) apricot yogurt

¾ cup plus 2 tbsp.–1 cup (200–250ml)
   unsweetened orange juice

1 Put the apricots, yogurt, and orange juice into a blender or food processor and blend for 1 minute, or until smooth.

2 Chill well, then pour into two glasses and serve.

Serves 2, makes about 2 cups (450ml)

Raspberry Rascal Booster

Prep time: 5 minutes

2 cups raspberries, thawed if frozen, juices reserved

1 medium orange

2 tsp. thick honey

1 If using fresh raspberries, remove the hulls, then wash and pat the fruit dry with paper towels. Put two raspberries to the side for decoration and put the rest into a blender. If the fruit has been frozen, add the juices as well.

2 Peel the orange, removing as much of the white pith as possible. Chop the flesh roughly, discarding any seeds, and put into the blender. Add the honey. Blend until smooth, then pour into a glass, decorate with the raspberries, and serve immediately.

HEALTHY TIP

This refreshing drink is bursting with vitamin C and anthocyanins, which help strengthen blood vessels and boost your immune system.

Serves 1, makes 1¼ cups (300ml)

Cranberry and Mango Smoothie

Prep time: 5 minutes

1 ripe mango, pitted (see page 156)

1 cup cranberry juice

⅔ cup plain yogurt

1 Peel and roughly chop the mango and put into a blender with the cranberry juice. Blend for 1 minute.

2 Add the yogurt and blend until smooth, then serve.

HEALTHY TIP

If you're on a dairy-free diet or are looking for an alternative to milk-based products, swap the yogurt for soy yogurt. Soy is a good source of essential omega-3 and omega-6 fatty acids, and can help to lower cholesterol.

Serves 2

For the slice—Mango and Pineapple

Mangoes

1 Cut a slice to one side of the pit. Repeat on the other side.
2 Cut parallel lines into the flesh of one slice, almost to the skin. Cut another set of lines to cut the flesh into squares.
3 Press on the skin side to turn the fruit inside out, so that the flesh is thrust outward. Cut off the chunks as close as possible to the skin. Repeat with the other half.

Pineapples

1. Cut off the bottom and crown of the pineapple, and stand the fruit on a cutting board.
2. Using a medium-size knife, peel away a section of skin, going just deep enough to remove all or most of the hard, inedible "eyes" on the skin. Repeat all the way around.
3. Use a small knife to cut out any remaining traces of the eyes.
4. Cut the peeled pineapple into slices.

Mango and Oat Smoothie

Prep time: 5 minutes

⅔ cup plain yogurt

1 small mango, peeled, pitted
and chopped (see page 156)

2 tbsp. rolled oats

4 ice cubes

1 Put the yogurt into a blender. Reserve a little chopped mango for decoration, if you like, and add the remaining mango, oats, and ice cubes to the yogurt. Blend the ingredients until smooth. Serve immediately, decorated with the chopped mango.

TRY THIS

If you can't find a mango, use 2 nectarines or peaches, or heaped 1 cup soft seasonal fruits, such as raspberries, strawberries, or blueberries, instead.

Serves 2

Summer Berry Smoothie

Prep time: 10 minutes

2 large, ripe bananas,

⅔ cup plain yogurt

3⅓ cups fresh or frozen
    summer berries

1 Peel and chop the bananas, then put into a blender. Add the yogurt and ⅔ cup (150ml) water, then blend until smooth. Add the berries and blend to a puree.

2 Strain the mixture through a fine sieve into a large bowl, using the back of a ladle to press it through the sieve. Pour into six glasses and serve immediately.

HEALTHY TIP

If you don't want to use summer berries, use iron- and fiber-rich apricots instead. Use either six ripe apricots, 16 ready-to-eat dried apricots, or 1 can (15-oz./425g) apricots in natural juice.

Serves 6, makes about 3½ cups (900ml)

For the Slice—Ginger

1. **Grating** Peel a large section of the ginger root with a vegetable peeler and cut off any soft brown spots.
2. Using a wooden or fine metal grater resting on a small plate or bowl, grate the ginger. Discard any large fibers adhering to the pulp.

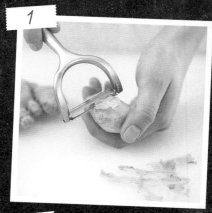

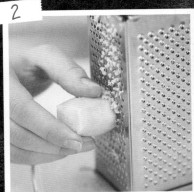

3 **Chopping** Cut slices off the ginger root and cut off the skin carefully and remove any soft brown spots. If you need very large quantities, you can peel a large section with a vegetable peeler before slicing.

4 Stack the slices and cut into shreds of the required thickness. To make dice, stack the shreds and cut to the required size.

5 **Pressing** If you need just the juice, cut thick slices off the ginger root and cut off the skin carefully, taking care to remove any soft brown spots under the skin. If you need very large quantities, you can peel a large section with a vegetable peeler. Cut the slices into chunks, then press with a garlic press over a small bowl to catch the juice.

4

Fruity Carrot with Ginger

TAKE 5

Prep time: 10 minutes

2 oranges

½in. (1cm) piece of fresh ginger, peeled and roughly chopped

⅔ cup (150ml) freshly pressed apple juice or 2 apples, juiced

⅔ cup (150ml) freshly pressed carrot juice or 3 medium carrots, juiced

mint leaves to decorate

1 Using a sharp knife, cut a slice of orange and put it aside for decoration. Peel the oranges, removing as much of the white pith as possible. Chop the flesh roughly, discarding any seeds, and put into a blender. Add the ginger.

2 Pour in the apple and carrot juices and blend until smooth. Divide between two glasses, decorate with quartered orange slices and a mint leaf and serve.

HEALTHY TIP

This drink is full of vitamin C and betacarotene, an antioxidant that helps combat harmful free radicals and promotes healthy skin, making it a great immunity-boosting supplement. Fresh ginger is good for calming an upset stomach and providing relief from bloating and gas.

Serves 2, makes 2½ cups (600ml)

Apple Crush

1 cup strawberries

⅔ cup (150ml) freshly pressed apple
juice or 2 apples, juiced

fresh mint leaves to decorate

1 Remove the hulls from the strawberries, then wash and pat the fruit dry with paper towels. Put on a tray and freeze for 40 minutes, or until firm.

2 When ready to serve, put the frozen strawberries into a blender and pour in the apple juice. Blend until smooth and slushy. Pile into a serving glass and decorate with mint leaves.

TRY THIS

Try raspberries instead of strawberries for a fruity variation on this refreshing drink.

Serves 1, makes 1¼ cups (300ml)

Strawberry and Camomile Comforter

Prep time: 5 minutes, plus infusing and cooling

2 camomile teabags

2in. (5cm) piece cinnamon stick

1 cup strawberries

⅔ cup (150ml) freshly pressed apple
   juice or 2 large apples, juiced

1 Put the teabags and cinnamon stick into a small heatproof container and pour in ⅔ cup (150ml) boiling water. Infuse for 5 minutes, then discard the bags and cinnamon stick. Cool.

2 When ready to serve, remove the hulls from the strawberries, then wash and pat dry the fruit with paper towels. Put into a blender.

3 Pour in the apple juice and cold camomile tea and blend for a few seconds until smooth. Pour into two tall glasses and serve.

TRY THIS

Camomile teabags are very convenient and easy to use, but freshly dried camomile flowers will give a stronger flavor.

Serves 2, makes 2 cups (600ml)

327 cal ♥ 8g protein
15g fat (3g sat) ♥ 5g fiber
44g carb ♥ 0.1g salt

8

254 cal ♥ 6g protein
14g fat (2g sat) ♥ 3g fiber
29g carb ♥ 0g salt

10

279 cal ♥ 10g protein
6g fat (1g sat) ♥ 5g fiber
49g carb ♥ 0.2g salt

12

208 cal ♥ 7g protein
9g fat (trace sat) ♥ 3g fiber
28g carb ♥ 0g salt

16

187 cal ♥ 2g protein
1g fat (0g sat) ♥ 4g fiber
47g carb ♥ 0.1g salt

28

192 cal ♥ 3g protein
1g fat (trace sat) ♥ 3g fiber
45g carb ♥ 0.1g salt

30

300 cal ♥ 5g protein
19g fat (11g sat) ♥ 1g
fiber 29g carb ♥ 1g salt

34

393 cal ♥ 4g protein
23g fat (14g sat) ♥ 0.8g fiber
47g carb ♥ 0.7g salt

48

206 cal ♥ 9g protein
10g fat (6g sat) ♥ 1g fiber
20g carb ♥ 0.8g salt

52

180 cal ♥ 4g protein
6g fat (4g sat) ♥ 0.9g fiber
27g carb ♥ 0.1g salt

54

449 cal ♥ 21g protein
40g fat (19g sat) ♥ 0g fiber
1g carb ♥ 1g salt

66

835 cal ♥ 29g protein
79g fat (46g sat) ♥ 0g fiber
1g carb ♥ 2.8g salt

68

453 cal ♥ 22g protein
25g fat (6g sat) ♥ 3g fiber
38g carb ♥ 1.6g salt

70

440 cal ♥ 14g protein
36g fat (29g sat) ♥ 0.7g
fiber 17g carb ♥ 1.8g salt

72

193 cal ♥ 9g protein
8g fat (1g sat) ♥ 2g fiber
22g carb ♥ 0.3g salt

8

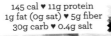

145 cal ♥ 11g protein
1g fat (0g sat) ♥ 5g fiber
30g carb ♥ 0.4g salt

20

188 cal ♥ 4g protein
7g fat (1g sat) ♥ 3g fiber
29g carb ♥ 0g salt

24

156 cal ♥ 1g protein
0g fat ♥ 2g fiber
40g carb ♥ 0g salt

26

376 cal ♥ 5g protein
25g fat (14g sat) ♥ 1g fiber
35g carb ♥ 0.7g salt

8

60 cal ♥ 2g protein
1g fat (0.1g sat) ♥ 0.5g
fiber 12g carb ♥ 0.2g salt

40

140 cal ♥ 3g protein
5g fat (3g sat) ♥ 0.9g fiber
22g carb ♥ 0.7g salt

42

49 cal ♥ 0.8g protein
3g fat (0g sat) ♥ 0g fiber
6g carb ♥ 0.1g salt

44

137 cal ♥ 4g protein
1g fat (trace sat) ♥ 2g fiber
31g carb ♥ 0.3g salt

6

218 cal ♥ 5g protein
2g fat (trace sat) ♥ 2g fiber
49g carb ♥ 0.5g salt

58

333 cal ♥ 4g protein
22g fat (11g sat) ♥ 1g fiber
31g carb ♥ 0.5g salt

60

233 cal ♥ 4g protein
8g fat (5g sat) ♥ 0.8g fiber
38g carb ♥ 0.4g salt

62

457 cal ♥ 23g protein
34g fat (17g sat) ♥ 2g fiber
17g carb ♥ 2.7g salt

76

263 cal ♥ 19g protein
21g fat (8g sat) ♥ 2g fiber
1g carb ♥ 0.7g salt

78

238 cal ♥ 23g protein
21g fat (5g sat) ♥ 6g fiber
2g carb ♥ 0.6g salt

80

149 cal ♥ 12g protein
12g fat (3g sat) ♥ 1g fiber
0g carb ♥ 0.3g salt

82

174 cal ♥ 14g protein
12g fat (3g sat) ♥ 2g fiber
2g carb ♥ 0.2g salt

86

122 cal ♥ 7g protein
7g fat (1g sat) ♥ 2g fiber
9g carb ♥ 0.3g salt

88

290 cal ♥ 9g protein
13g fat (6g sat) ♥ 4g fiber
39g carb ♥ 0.6g salt

94

125 cal ♥ 3g protein
6g fat (3g sat) ♥ 0.5g fiber
17g carb ♥ 0.7g salt

96

259 cal ♥ 8g protein
20g fat (9g sat) ♥ 0.5g
fiber 15g carb ♥ 0.7g salt

106

358 cal ♥ 8g protein
13g fat (7g sat) ♥ 0.5g fiber
54g carb ♥ 1.2g salt

108

175 cal ♥ 6g protein
4g fat (1g sat) ♥ 4g fiber
30g carb ♥ 0.5g salt

112

180 cal ♥ 5g protein
3g fat (1g sat) ♥ 1g fiber
34g carb ♥ 0.9g salt

114

429 cal ♥ 28g protein
20g fat (11g sat) ♥ 0.2g fiber
38g carb ♥ 3.1g salt

126

389 cal ♥ 17g protein
18g fat (10g sat) ♥ 2g fiber
41g carb ♥ 2.8g salt

128

384 cal ♥ 12g protein
31g fat (16g sat) ♥ 1g fiber
16g carb ♥ 1.9g salt

130

551 cal ♥ 32g protein
35g fat (22g sat) ♥ 1g fiber
27g carb ♥ 3.6g salt

132

172 cal ♥ 4g protein
1g fat (trace sat) ♥ 2g fiber
39g carb ♥ 0.2g salt

150

147 cal ♥ 5g protein
1g fat (trace sat) ♥ 8g fiber
39g carb ♥ 0.2g salt

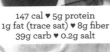

152

133 cal ♥ 4g protein
1g fat (trace sat) ♥ 2g fiber
29g carb ♥ 0.2g salt

154

145 cal ♥ 6g protein
2g fat (1g sat) ♥ 3g fiber
27g carb ♥ 0.2g salt

158

141 cal ♥ 5g protein
5g fat (1g sat) ♥ 0.8g fiber
20g carb ♥ 0.1g salt

8

50 cal ♥ 2g protein
1g fat (9g sat) ♥ 0.3g fiber
9g carb ♥ 0.1g salt

100

392 cal ♥ 4g protein
16g fat (9g sat) ♥ 0.5g fiber
48g carb ♥ 0.7g salt

102

207 cal ♥ 6g protein
8g fat (4g sat) ♥ 1g fiber
31g carb ♥ 0.8g salt

104

284 cal ♥ 15g protein
14g fat (5g sat) ♥ 2g fiber
26g carb ♥ 0.9g salt

8

137 cal ♥ 14g protein
9g fat (5g sat) ♥ 3g fiber
5g carb ♥ 0.4g salt

120

364 cal ♥ 15g protein
9g fat (2g sat) ♥ 8g fiber
55g carb ♥ 2.1g salt

122

331 cal ♥ 26g protein
25g fat (4g sat) ♥ 0g fiber
38g carb ♥ 3.1g salt

124

246 cal ♥ 12g protein
g fat (1g sat) ♥ 2g fiber
32g carb ♥ 0.4g salt

8

238 cal ♥ 16g protein
8g fat (1g sat) ♥ 2g fiber
25g carb ♥ 0.2g salt

140

205 cal ♥ 10g protein
3g fat (2g sat) ♥ 2g fiber
36g carb ♥ 0.3g salt

142

130 cal ♥ 9g protein
2g fat (1g sat) ♥ 1g fiber
24g carb ♥ 0.3g salt

148

108 cal ♥ 3g protein
g fat (trace sat) ♥ 3g fiber
24g carb ♥ 0.1g salt

0

128 cal ♥ 2g protein
1g fat (trace sat) ♥ 5g fiber
30g carb ♥ 0.1g salt

164

100 cal ♥ 1g protein
trace fat ♥ 1g fiber
24g carb ♥ 0g salt

166

52 cal ♥ 1g protein
trace fat ♥ 1g fiber
13g carb ♥ 0g salt

168

Index

PICTURE CREDITS
Photographers:
Marie-Louise Avery (page 115);
Neil Barclay (pages 77, 107 and
133); Steve Baxter (page 129);
Nicki Dowey (pages 9, 11, 13, 17,
19, 21, 23, 27, 29, 31, 57, 59, 61, 63,
73, 79, 83, 99, 123, 131, 139, 141, 149,
151, 153, 159, 161, 165, 167 and 169);
Will Heap (pages 81, 95 and 155);
Gareth Morgans (pages 67, 89 and
119); Myles New (pages 53 and
87); Craig Robertson (pages 15,
24, 25, 43, 47, 51, 74, 84, 92, 93, 109,
121, 136, 137, 156, 157, 162 and 163);
Lucinda Symons (pages 36, 37, 41,
45, 55, 69, 71, 97, 101, 103, 105, 113,
125 and 127); Kate Whitaker (pages
49 and 143).

Home Economists:
Anna Burges-Lumsden,
Joanna Farrow, Emma Jane Frost,
Teresa Goldfinch, Alice Hart,
Lucy McKelvie, Kim Morphew,
Aya Nishimura, Bridget Sargeson,
Stella Sargeson, Sarah Tildesley,
Kate Trend, Jennifer White and
Mar Mererid Williams.

Stylists: Tamzin Ferdinando,
Wei Tang, Sarah Tildesley,
Helen Trent and Fanny Ward.

CHEAP EATS

Budget-Busting Ideas That Won't Break the Bank

FLASH in the PAN

Spice Up Your Noodles & Stir-Fries

LET'S do BRUNCH

Mouth-Watering Meals to Start Your Day

PARTY FOOD

Delicious Recipes to Get the Party Started